Wild Animals

A very first picture book

Consultant: Nicola Tuxworth

LORENZ BOOKS

SYDNEY • LONDON • NEW YORK • BATH

Lion

A lion has a very
loud roar and sharp,
pointed teeth.

Chimpanzee

Chimpanzees carry their babies around with them. The baby has to hold on very tightly.

Giraffe

A giraffe's long neck helps it to reach the tops of tall trees. But ...

... bending down to drink is not so easy!

Crocodile

Crocodiles are fierce hunters. They can even stand up in rivers to catch birds to eat.

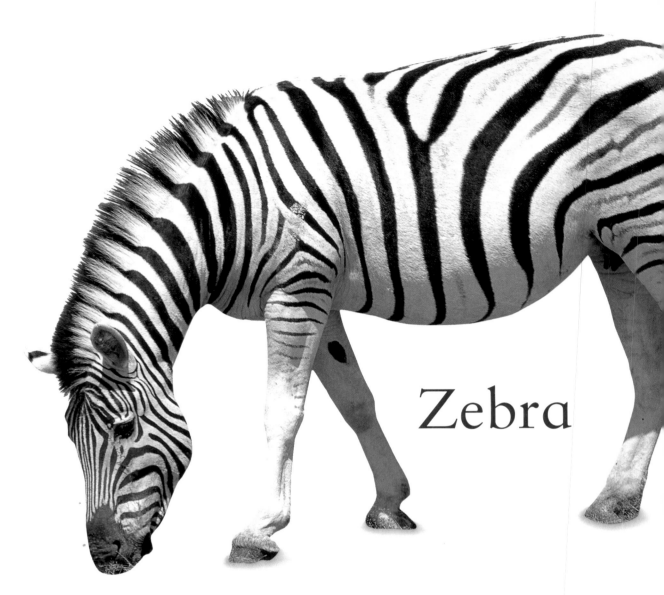

Zebra

A zebra
foal drinks
its mother's
milk.

Zebras live together
in big groups
called herds.

Polar bear

Polar bears live in
very cold places.

Polar bears have thick,
soft fur to keep them warm.
Baby polar bears
are called cubs.

Elephant

These elephants are thirsty. They suck water up with their long trunks, then squirt it down their throats.

Kangaroo

Kangaroos jump high into the air on their strong back legs.

Mummy kangaroos keep their babies safe in a special pocket called a pouch.

Penguin

Penguin families cuddle up
together to keep warm in the
snow and ice.

First published in 1996 by Lorenz Books

Lorenz Books is an imprint of
Anness Publishing Limited
Hermes House,
88-89 Blackfriars Road,
London SE1 8HA

Distributed in Canada by Raincoast Books
Distribution Limited

ISBN 1 85967 251 5

Publisher: Joanna Lorenz
Senior Children's Books Editor: Sue Grabham
Editor: Sophie Warne
Design and Typesetting:
    Michael Leaman Design Partnership

Picture credits: D Bruin/ZEFA, ZEFA-
Wisniewski, ZEFA-Pinto, H Reinhard/Bruce
Coleman Ltd, Zingel/ZEFA, G Ziesler/Bruce
Coleman Ltd, F Lanting/ZEFA-Minden,
J Simon/Bruce Coleman Ltd, ZEFA, Dr Eckart
Pott/Bruce Coleman Ltd, F Lanting/ZEFA-
Minden (2), ZEFA, J Foott/Bruce Coleman
Ltd, M Hoshino/ZEFA, J Balog/Tony Stone
Worldwide, Dr M P Kahl/Bruce Coleman
Ltd, F Prenzel/Tony Stone Worldwide,
J Cancalosi/Bruce Coleman Ltd (2), ZEFA-
Hummel, A Wolfe/Tony Stone Worldwide.

Printed in Spain by Artes Gráficas Toledo, S.A.
D.L. TO: 689-1997